Seasons of Grace

a devotional encouraging growth in the Lord

written and photographed
by
Hanna Lorraine

Copyright 2017 by Hanna Lorraine
All rights reserved.
Printed in the United States of America

Cover Text Illustration: Hanna Lorraine
Cover Design: Hanna Lorraine
Interior Design: Hanna Lorraine
Photographs: Hanna Lorraine

all scripture taken from the King James Version(KJV), public domain

Summer's Hope	4
Autumn's Grace	26
Winter's Patience	50
Spring's Strength	74

Summer's Hope

I was reading one morning in Matthew of the account where Peter was asked to get out of the boat and walk on water.

As it goes, he gets out and starts walking towards Jesus---who was also walking on the water. Within moments Peter's gaze catches the storm and rough winds around him.....(oh yeah, this was all taking place during a storm)....and filled with fear he begins to sink. Fortunately Jesus reached in and saved him. Afterwards Jesus asks the soaking wet and shaking Peter, "Why did you doubt?"

Haven't we all been there before? Where God asks us to do something seemingly crazy at the most inconvenient time? I mean Peter would've probably preferred this take place on a calm Sunday versus a stormy Tuesday.

Things like a change in careers, going back to school, adopting a child, starting a ministry, or relocating to another state can be asked of us, by God, when we least expect it...and sometimes at a time where nothing is calm or perfect. Whatever it is we've all been there.

So we get out of our boat. Suddenly our eyes catch a glimpse of everything that could go wrong if we continue on. Immediately we begin to sink in worry and doubt. The winds of failure seem to whip around us. Gasping for air we suddenly doubt our venture and begin to regret ever leaving our safe, little boat. Of course He immediately sends His word to lift us out of panic. Once we've caught our breath He asks, "Why did you doubt?"

Why did we doubt? We doubted because our focus was on what fear said could happen, instead of what faith said won't happen. We lost sight of our goal and let worry drag us down. We listened to the doubters of the world. We looked away from Him. So the next time He beckons you out of your comfortable and safe boat, don't look around, don't listen to the storm, don't look at your feet...look at Jesus and walk on the water.

F or the longest time I'd been fascinated with trying to own a Tiffany necklace. I felt like it was a necessity to being a woman, or at least a complete woman.
To me Tiffany jewelry separated the noticeable and beautiful women from the overlooked and average women.
And being overlooked and average was not my goal in life.
I was determined to not settle into non-existence, and this necklace was going to help me achieve that.
This necklace was going to open doors of acceptance, admiration, applause, and accolades for me.
As my search for the perfect Tiffany necklace went on, I stumbled upon an E bay listing of hundreds of Tiffany necklaces, all ranging from moderately high to very high prices. I paused at the site, baffled that so many women were finished with this highly valuable object.
I began to wonder how long each of them owned their necklaces...a day? a month? a year? Whatever the time frame, they were finished with it.
Whatever luster caught their eye was now gone, and all that remained were 11 bids and 14 days.
I then thought, how soon after I obtain this prize will I be tired of it, ready to cast it aside in regret? Perhaps the reason so many necklaces are up for bids is because they didn't fulfill the promise many women hoped for.
Perhaps the only doors that were opened were of comparison and insecurity, instead of acceptance and accolades.
As I exited the site, I was humbled and ashamed that I would stake my worth and life long happiness on a silver chain with a name I knew little about.
That night, in the red script on those delicate pages, I found my worth hidden in the name that is above every name.
A name that would open doors of freedom, grace, peace, and most of all love.
A name I can proudly wear without fear of regret later, and Who's value will remain priceless for ages to come.
That night I found a treasure worth having, Who's cost was already paid and Who's promises would never tarnish.

Set your affection on things above, not on things on the earth.

Colossians 3:2

Where can one find a perfect love?
A love that always anticipates, never hesitates, and is ever present....
A love that is relentless in the pursuit of the heart and never falls short in commitment and promise?
In the arms of a sweetheart we can seem pretty sure we have found it.
And in the care from our family we can feel oh so close to it.
Even through the devotion of dear friends, we can feel certain we're near to it.
But it wasn't until the red script on those delicate pages--stretched between two nails--reached into my starving heart, that I saw true Perfect Love....Jesus.
He is the only One who can fill that role in my life(to love me perfectly)a burden I should never lay on my spouse, family, or friends....for they can never love me perfectly, as I can never love them perfectly either.
But, Jesus.....well, He happily accepts the duty and does it flawlessly and effortlessly. And the more I become like Him, the more of His love they will get to experience through me. Even then my love will still not be perfect, and that's okay...because His love is perfect enough for all of us

Hereby perceive we the love of God, because he laid down his life for us

1 John 3:16

Unfortunately, I am that person....the one who is not fair with the marshmallow to cereal ratio. Whenever I start to pour the "magically deliciousness" I begin to control what is naturally suppose to come out on its own.

I cherry pick more rainbows, stars, hearts, the little blue things I haven't a clue what they are, and clovers.

I repeat this process until I feel I can be satisfied with my bowl.

What once held the illusion of an okay start to a day, quickly shattered to an equivalent of a bowl of pure sugar.

Not to mention, whoever goes after me will have far less rainbows and mystery blue pieces to enjoy. I need to quit this absurd habit!

I wonder how many of us are not happy with what lands in our "life bowl "?

The picture on the box promises rainbows, stars, and fun colorful surprises, but when poured, instead of being happy with the few rainbows that have landed, we become unsatisfied with the ratio.

So instead we begin to force the rainbows and stars into our bowl. Maybe it's another job, a better house, an attractive spouse, new clothes, a faster car, a better look, more likes, more attention, etc...

Let me give encouragement. Our bowl of life is not the only thing that will sustain us during the day and throughout our existence.

We can't control all the happiness that lands in it. Trying to force more rainbows into our lives only gives temporary fulfillment.

Because just like the actual cereal, it's gone and over with in just a couple of bites.

But what really sustains us is Jesus.

He's our nurture and our source of joy, in spite of the rainbow to cereal ratio. Don't force the rainbows and stars, but rather look to the One Who created them and has numbered them.

But seek ye first the kingdom of God, and his righteousness; and all these things shall be added unto you.

Matthew 6:33

It's not dead until He says it is.

Reflecting on the story of Jairus' daughter in Matthew 9, three things stand out to me. One, Jairus had urgently requested Jesus to heal his daughter to prevent her from dying. Two, when Jesus did not arrive to heal his daughter, she died and her father SAW and FELT that she was indeed dead...there was no disputing that there was no life left in her. And three, when Jesus arrived at Jairus' home He says that she was NOT DEAD but sleeping.

How many times have we seen the signs of a relationship about to die so we run to Jesus to save it? A mother-daughter relationship? A husband-wife relationship? A dear friendship? A son-father relationship? We get to Him as soon as we can before it's too late. However, time passes and we stand there watching all signs of life leaving this precious thing we've held so dear to us. We scramble within, grasping at any signs of life in our relationship to stay....but the last breath just leaves without any regard for our hopeful hearts. Stunned we fall apart, grieving the relationship we begged Jesus to save.

Let me encourage you just because it "looks" dead and "feels" dead does not mean it is truly dead, dead....at least not yet.

Believe me, Jesus heard your heart felt cry and He's seen your tears. Your request has not been ignored or brushed aside. When we call upon Jesus, we are calling upon the One Who is The Resurrection and the Life of, not only actual people, but of relationships as well. It's easy to assume all hope is lost when we're staring at no signs of life--when the communication has ceased or the feelings have grown cold....but it's not dead until He says it is. The thing I left out about the story is Jesus raised the little girl back to life and afterwards I'm pretty sure everyone glorified God for the miracle.

And so will you, when He brings you through this period of facing relational death. So, be at peace, Jesus has heard you and He is still the conqueror over all death. It's not dead until He says it is.

For we walk by faith, not by sight.

2 Corinthians 5:7

Pearls can take many, many years to form....sometimes twenty.

The process of transforming an ordinary piece of sand into a valuable jewel is remarkable, and seems almost bizarre.

Before we came to Jesus, we were just ordinary pieces of sand being washed to and fro without purpose. But then Jesus takes us and encapsulates us in His love and begins transforming us from an overlooked grain of sand, to a priceless pearl.

However the process is not complete overnight, as it starts very small.....mulling over every aspect of our lives--coating it and changing us little by little from sand to pearl.

It can seem like forever, until one day we start to finally see a slight resemblance to something shiny and glistening.

However, we're still not finished yet. There's plenty more mulling over, coating in His grace, and growing to do.

This process will not finish until we are in His glory. Right now we're living in the "pearl making phase".

This phase can seem frustrating as we struggle with still remaining imperfections in ourselves and others. But its important to remember we have not all arrived yet....I have not arrived yet. We're all still pearls in the making.

So today, I choose to extend grace to myself to recognize that as much as I'd like to be an all overcomer and get everything right, I'm still in the pearl making phase.

Also, I will extend the same grace to others I feel should be further along than myself.

Recognizing that judging their stage in the pearl phase is not only wrong but it's not truly representative of their growth.

Just because they got a head start on the process doesn't mean they shouldn't struggle with the same things I'm struggling with.

We're all being transformed. We're all in the process of changing from sand to pearl. We're all not finished yet.

And he said unto me, My grace is sufficient for thee: for my strength is made perfect in weakness.

2 Corinthians 12:8-9

One day I came across a roach the size of a cat......okay, maybe that's a slight exaggeration---it was the size of a hamster!

My first two thoughts were "How did this get in my house" and "I cannot let this beast just roam around my room." So I went after it with full force!

But the same determination I had for wanting it out was the same determination the roach had for wanting to stay.

Every lunge towards it sent the roach hiding in all sorts of places--behind my desk, in a shoe, behind the television, and under whatever it could find. This frustrating game of hide and seek went on for the longest 15-20 minutes!

This vile creature was faster than I had expected and more clever than I had anticipated.

Until, after another failed lunge at the horrid thing, I cried out loud, "God please help me, I can't do this on my own!" Not even a full 30 seconds passed before the roach emerged in front of me.

Without any hesitation, with the climax of an Arnold Schwarzenegger movie, I lifted up my foot(wearing a hefty outdoor slipper)and came down with all my might and obliterated the beast from this world, or my room at least. Victory was mine!

How often have we noticed something hideous in our lives that we've decided cannot stay any longer? It could be unforgiveness, a secret sin, self loathing, etc....

So we decide to go after it with all we have, but soon realize those buggers are way too clever, not wanting to leave, and hiding in sneaky places we hadn't considered: like our relationships, our home life, our job, or our thoughts. Exasperated we feel defeated because it looks like we'll never win.

Until the moment we call upon God to help. Immediately He assists and brings the foul thing under our heel, crushed and obliterated from our lives for good!

You see, I learned something from the roach fiasco: God cares about our desire to purge unwanted things from our lives.

He wants us to be victorious and understands our own human efforts can only go so far.

He's willing and waiting to help...all we need do is ask.

So the next time you go against a roach in your room, remember You have God as your weapon...not just your shoe, so use Him!

I can do all things through Christ which strengtheneth me.

Philippians 4:13

Our security is not found in our ability to hold onto Him.

For our mere human hands are not strong enough to hold tightly onto a Being Who's breath encapsulates the entire universe.

Trying to hold onto Him is like trying to capture the wind, in it's entirety, with a meager jar.

It's impossible and would be hard to prove that one even succeeded in capturing it.

But rather, our security lies within the binding grip of His love upon each of our lives.

It is His hand holding onto us, not us to Him, that preserves the promises breathed from His word.

It is His faithful grip upon our hearts that stirs us to seek Him, know Him, and commune with Him.

He has us……

And I give unto them eternal life; and they shall never perish,
neither shall any man pluck them out of my hand.
My Father, which gave them me, is greater than all; and no man is
able to pluck them out of my Father's hand.

John 10:28-29

I'm captivated by Moses' yearn and drive to pursue such a closeness with God, even when others were running away from Him. The people physically ran away from God, when He showed up in their midst, because they didn't understand Him.

They saw the darkness God was cloaking Himself in as a sign that He was something to avoid.

But Moses wasn't troubled by the darkness, for He knew the darkness was a temporary passage to where God was.

Sometimes we have to go through bouts of darkness to obtain a certain closeness with Him, that we otherwise would have never known.

For in that darkness, God is revealing a bigger glimpse of His character and illuminating a bigger part of Him we never knew we needed.

It's human nature to run away from God in fear, doubt, and anger when darkness descends....just look at our society.

However, in these dark times, let's not view the darkness as evidence that God should be avoided, but rather that He's using it to draw us closer into an unshakable closeness with Him.

Run to Him, not from Him.

But it is good for me to draw near to God: I have put my trust in the Lord God, that I may declare all thy works.

Psalm 73:28

Jesus allows us to see other's shortcomings and failures not so we can feel better about ourselves, but so that we may love them through it and in spite of it....with His love.

It's easy to feel a sense of pride and achievement to know we don't struggle with the same thing "so and so" does, but that attitude only magnifies our own "goodness" and not God's.

Our sense of greatness shouldn't be magnified in someone else's weakness. Having a grace centered attitude, instead of a judgmental/self righteous one, will allow us to be moved with His love and compassion when dealing with another person's shortcoming.

Brethren, if a man be overtaken in a fault, ye which are spiritual, restore such an one in the spirit of meekness; considering thyself, lest thou also be tempted.
Bear ye one another's burdens, and so fulfil the law of Christ.

Galatians 6:2

God's Word is the only assurance of self worth I can trust.

Forever reminding me what I'm made of and Who I'm made for. Constantly shattering false reflections of beauty and perfection.

Proving over and over again that to hate myself is to actually hate the One who made me.

Always showing me the venom in comparing myself to the smoke screened illusions of life being lived flawlessly.

And last, declaring my worth is not found in a series of numbers, a set of lists, a certain group, a shelf of awards, a pile of perfect pictures, or a million "at a boys".

How well we're keeping up with so and so, how we look compared to "so and so", how noticed we are, and how noticed we are for getting noticed are all empty distractions that never pay out.

Jesus. Jesus. Jesus. That's it. He is our true source of worth. The exchange rate is so astronomically in our favor---our starving heart for an abundance of everything He is and more!

The world can't fulfill that kind of promise....it tries but it never can.

He sealed our worth forever on the cross, so why are we still seeking it from a world that will one day fade away?

Chasing the world's applause will only lead to hopelessness.

But choosing to find worth in Jesus will lead to peace.

Yea, I have loved thee with an everlasting love:
therefore with lovingkindness have I drawn thee.

Jeremiah 31:3

Autumn's Grace

Abide.

I keep running across that word more frequently.
I think maybe we're in a day and age where Jesus is trying so desperately to remind us to abide in Him.
There's something about this present moment that is different from the generations past.
So many "I" centered focal points vying for hearts.
From products advertising "love yourself more", to articles on "how to become a better you", or inspiring commercials telling young people "show the world the real you". All of these point to the fruitless cultivation of abiding in one's self....lifting up one's self, trusting in one's self.
I can't love myself more if it's just with my own love.
Because I need Jesus' love to replace my broken love and wounded heart.
I can't become a better me with just my sheer willingness.
Because I need Jesus' strength of the cross reminding me that it is Him Who transforms me into His new creation and image.
And I can't show the world the real me without showing Jesus to them.....impossible.
However, to a world without Jesus, abiding in yourself seems like a fail proof platform to build one's life upon.
Focusing on one's greatness and praising one's self is the banner the world wants all to raise high.
I know Jesus is beckoning His children to lay down that banner, step away from the faulty platform, and readjust our focus on Him.
Because one day the praise will end, the platform will crumble, and the banner will be torn.
All that will be left are empty hearts holding an empty promise the world never intended to fill.
But Jesus......
But Jesus......
He's the everything the world is relentlessly trying to duplicate and replace, but can't.
Abide in Him.

I love fall leaves.

Their beautiful colors just amplify the sunshine in a way no other leaf can. But then I marveled at the fact that the reason these leaves were so beautiful is because they were in the process of dying.....and that got me thinking.

As a Christian I am taught that dying to myself and my selfish wants is a part of "walking the walk". But sometimes the process is uncomfortable.

However, what I never realized is that it can also be very beautiful.

The gorgeous colors of fall can only happen once the tree has yielded it's leaves to die.

And those vibrant colors are what allow the sun to shine through in the most glorious way.

The same process can be applied to me.

Once I've yielded those parts of myself to die, then the beautiful transformation of becoming more like Jesus can occur.

The vibrant colors of His will, His love, and His grace will begin to show. And once that starts, only then can His glorious light truly shine through me.

He must increase, but I must decrease.

John 3:30

In this world we all have come to know the sting of sadness and quite a few tears.
However, through Jesus I have come to understand that all those tears are indeed temporary.
Although it can feel like a lifetime, when the tears seem to never quit coming, they were never meant to stay forever.
Jesus has not given us an inheritance of eternal sorrow and forever tears.
Instead we have been given a promise that one day the tears will end....the sorrow will end.
That the tears that have stained our pillow at night will one day disappear, and the tears currently running down our face today will one day dry up.....for they are temporary, the pain and sadness are temporary.
In this world our temporary state of feeling the tears may linger longer than we would like, but it will not go on forever.
Our inheritance is one of wholeness and healing with abounding joy in the forever presence of Jesus, our Saviour, where the memory of those tears will haunt us no more.
These tears.
They aren't our forever lot or our final resting place.
So when the tears come take heart in this--they are temporary.

And God shall wipe away all tears from their eyes; and there shall be no more death, neither sorrow, nor crying, neither shall there be any more pain: for the former things are passed away.

Revelation 21:4

God's faithful and very detailed provision can be seen in His redemptive plan for mankind.

Long before the prophets spoke of it, He was setting up every key detail needed to bring it about.

From the desire of a man to open an inn and a stable in a small town in Israel. The birth of a donkey, who would be sold at a price a young pregnant couple could afford for their long journey.

To the silver smith who would mold out the silver coins used years later to betray a friend.

The seamstress who would weave a garment straight through without any seams... to be purchased by a carpenter's son, and later fought over at an execution site.

A just man eyeing a cave in a garden, with the foresight of it being his final resting place...but later giving it up for a great teacher.

To the wheat growing in a field and made into bread to be broken at a Passover meal--where 12 common men gathered.

The purple dye from the sea used to make a majestic robe for an officer, but instead it would drape a King in mockery.

And finally the young tree sapling growing strong in the sunshine, to be cut down into beams a hundred years later and erected on a hill, displaying the ultimate sacrifice for the world to see.

Every detail of the redemptive plan, monumental and small, was carefully orchestrated by a God Who's one track goal was to save His precious creation from the grip of sin and death.

Every detail and every piece mattered.

Our God is a God of details.

But God commendeth his love toward us, in that, while we were yet sinners, Christ died for us.

Romans 5:8

How can I speak of Your light without first telling of the darkness I once walked in?
How can I speak of Your healing without mentioning the pain I endured?
How can I speak of Your comfort without sharing the moments of loneliness I went through?
How can I speak of Your provision without showing the near empty jar of oil?
How can I speak of Your love without remembering a starving heart searching in all the wrong places?
And How can I speak of Your forgiveness without the memory of wrongs being made right?
For me to speak of knowing You, I must first speak of my needing You.
Because it was in my many needs of You, that I tasted and saw that You are indeed Oh, so good.

O taste and see that the Lord is good.

Psalm 34:8

Thinking about how nervous David must have been choosing a bag full of rocks, just after declaring he would defeat Goliath. I wonder if for a moment his nerves rattled him. Either way we know how the story goes...he defeats the giant with one whirling rock from his sling. Sounds crazy....and even sounds reckless. But that's that kind of faith we're suppose to have--the crazy reckless kind.
The kind that doesn't hesitate to face head on difficulties or giants in our midst. The kind that fully trusts in God's ability working through us, no matter how off kilter a situation seems. You see David's victory wasn't in the type of rock he chose or his technique in slinging it. He understood fully putting his faith in these alone would make him a dead man.
He needed God to stand together with him to face Goliath.....and God did. The moment David's faith transferred off of his abilities and tools and onto God, the victory became his. So it didn't matter how high or how imperfect David's form was slinging that rock....the moment the rock left the sling Goliath didn't stand a chance--because God was that rock.
David knew that God was His real weapon, not a sack of rocks or a sling. Although God used them to humble a nation and defeat a giant, David understood that the victory came from God. So it's not in what we can do, what tools we have, what we can't do, or what we don't have that determines the victory.
It's our faith and absolute trust in God's abilities that propels Him to knock down the giants we face everyday. He may use something odd or weird to get the job done, but the force and precision needed comes straight from Him. He's our rock amidst the other rocks in our sack, but in reality He should be the only rock we reach for.

Then said David to the Philistine, Thou comest to me with a sword, and with a spear, and with a shield: but I come to thee in the name of the Lord of hosts

1 Samuel 17:45

My struggle.

I have what I call Charlie Brown syndrome...let me explain. Like Charlie Brown, I too am always trying to finally kick that metaphorical football. Many times a day that football appears. It appears in the form of challenges, new tasks, unexpected demands, the sudden call to perform, and ill timed vulnerability. Kicking this football is important. Failure in any of these areas is not an option. So there I see it, the football. I am determined to kick it. I get all energized, I fix my eyes on the ball, I tell myself this is it.....then I take off running towards the football.

No sooner I start I immediately fumble, tripping over my feet, rolling in the air, and falling on my face in a graceless fashion. I'm embarrassed. Hurt. Disappointed. Angry with myself. And feeling oh so low.

Once again I've failed. Once again I've fallen. Once again my best wasn't good enough. The after shock is so profound that it echoes into the rest of my day, leaving me without the confidence to even change a toilet paper roll.

Has anyone ever been there? This is a struggle I deal with on a daily basis because I'm not elegant. I'm not cutting edge. I don't easily catch on. And I'm not the poster face of a winner.

However, when I open His word, I am told differently. My flaws and shortcomings vanish in the red script of His loving words. My insecurities and list of failures disappear in His grace filled promises. And my tears of disappointment He wipes away with new mercies each day. I may never kick that football, however I know He's still cheering me on anyway and loving me just as I am. Tomorrow I'll try again.

...for my strength is made perfect in weakness.

2 Corinthians 12:9

I wonder what Moses' mother's thoughts were when she laid her son in the river.

She had worked so hard to conceal him all those months. She did her best to hide him and handle the matter herself. But now it was obvious, the task had outgrown her efforts and had become too big for her to do on her own. The only thing she could do was build a basket and set him free upon unknown waters into the hands of God.

How often have we been there? Where we've handled a situation on our own, but now it seems to have gotten too big for our hands. We've done our best to conceal our silent efforts, only to realize we can't do it anymore. Whether it's a circumstance at work, a relationship, or something else. Whatever it is we've exhausted all our efforts, prayed all the prayers, and have given all we got. What then? The only thing we can do is let it go into our Father's hands. Set it free from our nervous grip onto the waters of His will.

It can seem scary to release our circumstance or relationship into His hands, especially when we've invested so much into making it work.

But we're not just releasing it out into the unknown, we're sending it into the hands of an ever faithful and capable God--one who knows how to move past our limitations and bring our circumstance or relationship into His perfect will. So be at peace and know He can take it from here.

Have faith in God

Mark 11:22

The hardship you are experiencing today is allowing you to know a characteristic of God that otherwise you would have had a hard time understanding on your own. What part of Himself is He trying to make known to you? Is it that He is your provider?....Your healer? Your comforter? Your sustainer? Your deliverer? Or perhaps your father? Whatever it is, He is actively revealing a vital part of Himself through your hardship. Whatever He's revealing to you is exactly what you need to make it through your hardship. And whatever you're going through is exactly what you need in order to experience that particular nature of Him.

As difficult as it appears, learning to kiss the wave that slams us into Him will enable us to go deeper into fellowship with Him, not only in the calm times but in the rough times.

And we know that all things work together for good
to them that love God, to them who are the called
according to his purpose.

Romans 8:28

Insecurity is such a rising epidemic.

It sucks the marrow of who God says we are right out of our bones, making us fragile and susceptible to crumbling under society's unbearable standards.

Before we know it, we're no longer pillars of His declaring strength, but dusty ruins testifying that we were no more cherished than a pile of stones.

But I know that isn't truth.

For I am cherished, I am loved, I am purposeful, I am not forsaken, and I was declared into being by a God Who only creates beautiful things.

So, so what if the lie of comparison is the norm? Stand tall in the red script of His loving, ever faithful, and ever true words. Cling to His declaring love and truth spoken over you.

Know who you are, and most importantly Who's you are.

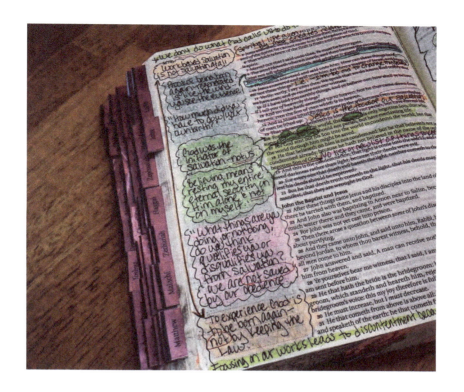

But ye are a chosen generation, a royal priesthood, an holy nation, a peculiar people; that ye should shew forth the praises of him who hath called you out of darkness into his marvellous light

1 Peter 2:9

I cannot abide in myself alone. I lack all the components needed to sustain my being.

If I try to root myself within myself, I will inevitably find that I'm just as the walking dead....no life, no radiance, no purpose.

My only chance of not only surviving, but thriving, is to make myself one with You.....to latch hold onto the Vine of Your Word, letting it completely engulf my will--like a vine overtaking a neglected wall.

So that to the untrained eye, it would be difficult to see where You begin and I end.

I am the vine, ye are the branches: He that abideth in me, and I in him, the same bringeth forth much fruit: for without me ye can do nothing.

John 15:5

Thy will.

I look all around me and see all of Your creation yielding themselves to Your will.

The trees change leaves with each new season.

The ocean comes up only so far onto land.

The bees pollinate the fruit trees and all the flowers.

The birds keep the insects in check and help disperse seeds for new plant growth.

The stars give light at night, and the sun never fails to give us day.

If all of these artifacts of Your hand can yield themselves to Your will....to follow it and carry it out with unceasing devotion and without delay,

Then how can I, who was made a little lower than the angels, whom You call Your child....do anything less than full hearted submission to Your will?

If a mere ant can give You pleasure by fulfilling Your will, then what joyous smile will it be to Your heart to see Your child actively living the will for her?

Now the God of peace, that brought again from the
dead our Lord Jesus, that great shepherd of the sheep,
through the blood of the everlasting covenant,
Make you perfect in every good work to do his will,
working in you that which is wellpleasing in his sight,
through Jesus Christ; to whom be glory for ever and
ever.

Hebrews 13:20-21

Winter's Patience

T is the season of hope.

There are many people in the world who feel they are without hope.
That life has passed them by and there isn't a hand left to save them.
The bottom of a pit is the hardest place to believe that hope exists....I know because I've been there.
I've sat there with my head hung low with nothing but despair to comfort me.
The feeling of failure mixed with loneliness is enough to suffocate one's will to thrive.
But I'm here to testify that Hope is very much alive and vibrant, even in the darkest spot.
When Hope first arrived over 2,000 years ago, it came in one of the darkest times in history, where tyranny and captivity reigned.
It was delivered to a people who believed they would always be the conquered and never the victor.
The arrival of Hope signified the beginning of light reigning over darkness.
Hope would grow to teach them the value of faith during storms, the power of love and forgiveness over hate, and a plan greater than what their eyes could see.
That even in the midst of despair and failure, Hope promised to walk with them through their tears...to be their breath and strength.
No longer would they have to be alone. Jesus came to be that hope....and He was that hope for me....and He can be that hope for you too.
Your circumstances may not change and your pit may still be quite deep.
But with Jesus the darkness that surrounds you will be replaced with His light of peace and comfort.
The loneliness of failure will vanish, leaving behind the fragrance of redemption and grace.
Corrie Ten Boom said it simply, "No pit is so deep that He is not deeper still."
Hope is alive and is nearer than you know. Please don't give up.

Praying through tears.

It's as though you've exasperated all the words you can, and all that's left are the tears. The tears themselves take up where your words left off and lunge themselves further into heaven's realm, desperately searching answers to "why" "when" and "how long". Take comfort, Jesus sees your tears. Every one of them is known by Him. Your ache inside for answers is ever before Him. You are not crying alone. You are not searching alone.

He is with you and cherishes your tears....not one of them goes unnoticed or unaccounted for. He knows the reasons and He knows the "why".

And one day your tears will testify of His goodness and faithfulness through these dark moments. But until then take comfort, He's heard you and He's seen you....but most importantly He's got you.

The Lord is nigh unto them that are of a broken heart;
and saveth such as be of a contrite spirit.

Psalm 34:18

Joy...is what this season represents.

From magazine ads, holiday movies, and greeting cards...if ever there was a time joy was promised, it's during this season. But the saddening reality is no matter how much we force it, how much we pay for it, or give for it, true joy cannot be bought or bargained for.
Why? Because joy doesn't glimmer and shine with false hope.
Instead it came wrapped in the swaddling cloth of love, laid in the promise of redemption, and hidden in our consuming darkness.
The night Joy entered our shadowy world, the heavens couldn't contain their excitement! For once, humanity had a chance....
for once our path could be made straight.....
for once there was light again.
Joy would soon have other names join it, like Counselor, Healer, Comforter, and finally Savior.
But for now, on that night, there was Joy....Joy for all mankind--our redemption had finally come! Joy will never be found in packages and stores. Instead you'll find it freely given for all, lying in a manger

Looking unto Jesus the author and finisher of our faith;
who for the joy that was set before him endured the cross,
despising the shame, and is set down at the right hand of
the throne of God.

Hebrews 12:2

Do you feel downcast and forgotten? There is someone who longs to comfort you and hold you through this season in your life...Jesus. Jesus has been there....He's heard your cries, He's seen your cast down spirit, He's felt your pain in the lonely nights. He beckons you to come to Him.
Throw yourself into His arms. Let your tears fall onto His ever capable shoulders. Let His arms wrap you up in His abounding love.
Let the soothing hushes of His healing lullaby gently take the pain from your heart. And let His gracious faithfulness tuck you into His peaceful rest. Please go to Him, don't suffer alone anymore. He's ever waiting with arms open just for you. Please go to Him.

Come unto me, all ye that labour and are heavy laden,
and I will give you rest.

Matthew 11:28

The drummer boy is a story I've grown up with.

Its simple message of giving from the heart has echoed into our Christmas season for many years.

Here we have a poor boy who's life's wanderings lead him to the stable where baby Jesus laid. Compelled to give a gift, he soon realizes he doesn't have anything of worth to give the baby....after all, he was poor.

As the story goes, he decides the only thing he can give is a song played on his drums. His song ends up being the most valued gift presented, becoming a lullaby we sing every Christmas.

Fable or fact, this story has a powerful message that is as plain as day.

Once we find ourselves in the presence of the Savior, overcome by awe and gratitude, the only thing we need bring is our hearts.

The beat of gratitude within our hearts is the melody that embodies true praise.

As insignificant as it may seem, our grateful hearts become the only gift of value in His eyes.

He values our hearts more than any talent, sacrifice, or deed we could possess.

A grateful heart can see the miracle of God's gift in the manger as so much more than just a baby having been born.

It allows us to comprehend the majesty of God's mercy and grace bestowed freely to all.

In doing so, we humbly confess that our good efforts will always fall short of His glory. And thus reveal to us our desperate need of Him.

So this season isn't about giving our best to Him but rather the giving of ourselves...just as we are.

...for the Lord seeth not as man seeth; for man looketh on the outward appearance, but the Lord looketh on the heart.

1 Samuel 16:7

Yea though I....

Yea though I walk in uncertainty and darkness, I will will not stumble nor fall, for You are a lamp unto my feet and a light onto my path.

Yea though I wear the cloak of loneliness--where friend and family are far from me, then in You will I find comfort...for You are a friend which sticketh closer than a brother.

Yea though I witness my dreams sink to the bottom of the sea, and my hopes dashed on the rocks, then in You I will find strength for a new day. For in You I draw my sustenance and meaning for life.

Yea though I live in the land of the plenty one day and in the barren desert the next, my soul will not anguish nor fret....for You are my supplier of all my needs.

And Yea though I walk through the valley of the shadow of death, I will fear no evil, for You are with me.

Every "yea though I" in the past and every "yea though I" to come, You have and will continue to be ever faithful. For You are the joy of my salvation and so, so good.

Yea though I....

Yea though I....

Yea though I....

I can face every one without fear for Your ever present faithfulness has never failed me.

And because of it, it is well with me.

God is faithful

1 Corinthians 1:9

When I was pregnant with my second child, I had a bad night of pre-term contractions.

It was difficult for me to move. I wasn't sure how I was going to get from the kitchen chair to my bedroom on the other side of the house.

Then without hesitation and without me having asked, my hubby stopped his stirring of dinner on the stove, turned to me, and scooped me up into his arms. Before I could register what was happening, I was moving through the house, upon his arms, and gently to our bedroom.

How he arrived at that decision to carry me across the house, I don't know....all I know is that at that moment I needed to be carried. And I believe his deep love for me knew that was the only option.

Feeling humbled, in pain, and so dearly cared for, my eyes welled with tears that such a person as he would love me so, so much--to carry me to where I could not bring myself.

This demonstration of selfless love from my husband was, to me, a mirrored image of Jesus' love for us.

Sometimes we reach a point in our lives where the pains of our world become too much to bear, thus keeping us immobilized and stuck in pain.

But then here comes Jesus, Who never needed to be beckoned and Who is fully aware of our limitations. Stooping down, He gently scoops us up in His loving arms and brings us to the place we could not bring ourselves.

Where is the place you're desperately trying to get to but you just can't because it hurts too much?

Is it a place of reaching true forgiveness?

A place of finally feeling self worth?

A place where the fear of tomorrow won't be there?

A place of letting go the past once and for all?

Or a place you can finally rest?

Whatever it is that you're longing to be, but can't for the pain you're suffering, know this--Jesus' deep, genuine love for you is capable of finishing the journey for you....with you in His ever caring arms.

He's there...He's always been there, and He longs to carry you.

Come unto me, all ye that labour and are heavy laden, and I will give you rest.
Take my yoke upon you, and learn of me; for I am meek and lowly in heart: and ye shall find rest unto your souls.
For my yoke is easy, and my burden is light.

Matthew 11:28-30

"And suddenly there was with the angel a multitude of the heavenly host praising God, and saying, Glory to God in the highest, and on earth peace, good will toward men." This well known verse in the Bible marks the turning point in the story of mankind's redemption.

I love a good book any day, but I have a problem with wanting to find out the ending right away. I become too invested in the characters and too emotionally involved. Because of this I tend to cheat and read the ending first.

I know this is completely wrong, but I can't help wanting to know if there will be a happy ending. Well, this same logic can be found in the Bible.

In Isaiah it tells us that God knew the end, or the ending, from the beginning. Meaning, from the first page of mankind---where man fell from grace, God skipped ahead and wrote the ending....an ending where sin and death are finished forever. Where we will live with Him for all eternity and every tear will be wiped away. This ending He foresaw from the very beginning. However getting there---the middle of the story, would take some character and plot development for many chapters to come. Until finally, we read where the angels are singing in the heavens because of what God has done. Here, the climax of the story begins. The nucleus of the plot is unveiled taking an interesting turn---God in human form descends as a baby to live among mankind.

In doing so He will learn the weaknesses and strengths of being human, as well as the sorrows and struggles.

Until finally, He will offer Himself as the final payment for all sin. Thus redeeming mankind from eternal separation.

So whenever I read about the angels rejoicing, it makes my heart soar with excitement! God, the author and finisher of our faith, was in the process of making a way for there to be a happy ending...and for that I am so grateful!

Behold, a virgin shall be with child, and shall bring forth a son, and they shall call his name Emmanuel, which being interpreted is, God with us.

Matthew 1:23

The holidays have a nucleus of family at the center. It's the time of year when we reach out to members far and near, when we take the time to let loved ones know how much we cherish them, and when we reflect on memories passed with hopes of new ones in the future.
However, this time of year can be very sorrowful when there are torn relationships, unresolved rifts, and bitter memories instead.
I just want to give a bit of encouragement if you're finding yourself facing the bleak reality of strained or cut off relationships this season.
Jesus sees your pain.
He experienced the longing for reconciliation from the pinnacle of the cross.
He mapped out the distance between bitterness and forgiveness with His outstretched arms.
And He felt the tears of loneliness in that dark 9th hour.
You're not going through this alone. He's there holding you when the aching to send a card or a present to that loved one hits you in the store aisle. And He's there beside you when that Christmas song comes on the radio and you want so desperately to call that person in your heart.
He's there, He sees, He's aware, and He wants you to continue to love that person...unconditionally.
Jesus exampled true love in its unconditional form for us to follow.
He gave His love without expecting anything in return, not even the smallest positive sign of reciprocation from the other person.
That means loving faithfully, even in the midst of never seeing a return on your love from the other person.
True unconditional love feels one sided at times, and almost unfair.
Jesus knew the whole time the love He poured out would be rejected by many, but He still chose to pour it out freely upon everyone.
His example is an example I believe we all can follow, especially during the holiday season.
So, just take a breath, cry at night to the Christmas song, and choose to truly love that person this season...even if all you get in return is silence.
Remember Jesus is there with you during this painful time, and He's your perfect example.
You can do this, because He already has.

Thou shalt love thy neighbour as thyself.

Mark 12:31

Lately I've been soaking in the words "God is my Father", and the massive implications of its meaning. The Bible speaks of us having been adopted or grafted into His family....thereby making Him our Father. But it wasn't until I looked deeper at what adoption really meant....at least the adoption He was referring to, that I finally understood its meaning. You see, here on earth we can only adopt by name and through name only....that's the most we can do. And even then it doesn't erase the true biological identity from the child's life. However when God spoke of adoption, He went above and beyond--way further than we could ever do. He not only reached out and adopted us through name, but He sealed our identity with Him by also adopting us through blood--His blood. His blood completely changed our spiritual DNA to match His. No longer would we be associated with our former "biological identity", because our new blood points only to God as our real Father.

Our hereditary gene of death and destruction were destroyed and a new gene of righteousness and abounding life took its place. We became truly His! However the enemy tries relentlessly to prick us with lies that we really don't belong to God...that our adoption isn't legal and we'll never truly fit into His family....eventually the truth will come out that we're outsiders. But the minute that liar pricks us, the blood of Jesus will flow through us--testifying that we are indeed a child of God. Every drop shouts that we are His and only His forever and ever. And no one can ever come against it or disprove it. The proof will always be in The Blood!

Behold, what manner of love the Father hath bestowed upon us, that we should be called the sons of God

1 John 3:1

One step.

Then another.

Another step.

One more step.

Another step.

So often the healing in our hearts is slow occurring.

We'd like to think we can spring out of pain like a jack rabbit on a trampoline, but in reality it's more like a slow moving turtle in thick mud. We look around and see everyone else leaping and bounding over hurtles, while we're still trying to get momentum.

Don't be discouraged if this is you. We all can't get ourselves out of the mucky pain by ourselves, sometimes we have to be lifted out by Him.

This doesn't mean you've failed or are weak, because you're not.

It just points to the truth that we can't do it alone, especially when it involves a wounded heart.

So if you're a wounded heart still struggling for healing, be still and know He's got you and will lift you higher and farther from the pain than you could've imagined.

He healeth the broken in heart, and bindeth up their wounds.

Psalm 147:3

The presents have been given, the eggnog all drank, gift receipts sorted, extra batteries purchased, and Auld Lang Syne heard at midnight.
Now all that's left is a trip into the attic to gather the red and green bins that house the tinsel and lights the other 330 days a year.
With each take down of holiday bliss, and each commercial offering tips on a better year and better you, let's remember one important thing:
God is.
Meaning whatever we'll be striving to be or perfect this year, God is already that "thing" we're striving for.
Whether it's more patience, more self control, a better outlook on life, a deeper sense of forgiveness, a willingness to serve, the ability to let go, or the faith to make the jump into something new....God is already that thing you're chasing after for this new year.
He's already supplied your goal through Him and Him alone.
He is the completion to any void you need filling, He's the remedy to any healing you're searching for, He's the leap of faith you're hoping for, and He's the transformation to self you're striving for.
Whatever your goal for this year is....God is.
As we disassemble the tree and take down the lights, let's take our well meaning goals with stride remembering He is the answer to our need.

But my God shall supply all your need according to his riches in glory by Christ Jesus.

Philippians 4:19

Spring's Strength

He tore the veil....

To tear something requires a devotion to seeing a whole object split apart, with the full use of one's strength, hands, and teeth if need be.

The veil that hung in the temple was hung there by mankind for protection from the presence of God. That veil manifested the moment mankind sinned, which meant we could no longer fellowship with God.

It stood as a visual reminder that God was on one side, and mankind on the other.....separated, isolated, and unreachable for relationship. Sadly, it remained like this for many, many centuries. However, I believe the instant Jesus breathed His last, and the promise of the cross was fulfilled, that God ran....to the veil! I believe He didn't wait another nano second of history, but rather He ran with all His might to the temple to tear that veil! He took that veil with both His hands--hands used to fashion the entire universe, used all of His strength--strength used to defeat an entire Egyptian army, and maybe even His teeth, and tore that veil apart!

He was determined that veil was to no longer remain in place.

He didn't want one more moment of being separated from the mankind He so desperately loved. He didn't want one more second of us standing isolated, and Him unreachable.

It was over, It was finished.....It was done.

And the loving part is, He didn't make us tear it down ourselves...although it was our fault why we had to hang it up to begin with. No, He decided to do it Himself because His fervent, ever chasing love couldn't stand another moment away from us.

So He did it with His own two hands.....He tore the veil!

Created with purpose. Fashioned with intent.
Molded by design.
These are the words engraved upon each of us.
Our first breath ignited a firework of possibilities--illuminating a future full of promise.
We were set in motion by choice, not accident, by the very Creator of the universe. His fashionable hands brought forth a dream of someone who would come to know the heights and depths of His abounding love.
That someone is both you and I. We were His dream, we were His choice, we were His masterpiece.
So be encouraged, the God who created you did not make a mistake.
Nor did He make you inferior. You were made with a raging love and a fierce devotion to see you flourish in His will. Not one detail about you was overlooked, under thought, or ignored. You are the blended, beautiful handiwork of the One who creates only good things.
You are purposeful.
You are valuable.
You are needed.
And you are wanted...you are loved.

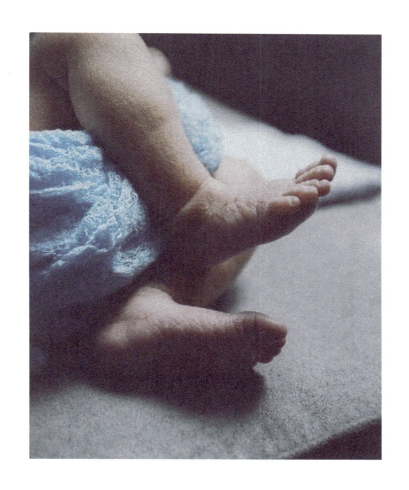

I will praise thee; for I am fearfully and wonderfully made

Psalm 139:14

I love how David puts it in Psalm 23--"The Lord is MY shepherd."

Oftentimes our insight can get skewed and we quote this famous chapter thinking of Jesus as The Shepherd or a Shepherd, but not absorbing that it's personal and possessive...He's MY shepherd and YOUR shepherd.

I know for me in the past, my view was that I was one of a million in His flock, and He was way, way, way in the front somewhere.....not really aware of little ole me in the back, trotting along, and trying not to get lost or pushed further in the back. And those in the front of the flock....wow, they must feel super close to Jesus....they don't need any faith! While I'm in the back with another sheep's rear end in front of me, relying on faith, memory verses, and trying to not look confused or left out.

Well, looking back, I can see how silly my view was. Jesus isn't a distant shepherd leading believers in rank like filing system, unaware of little stragglers in the back. No, He's a very personal and passionate shepherd who takes head counts, assesses the well being and conditions of each of us--one by one, and not only knows where we are in the flock, but knows us all by name. And to top it off, He walks beside each of us....not just with the few in the front.....no, each of us...at the same time---no favorites!

That means even me in the back....He's walking besides me, assessing me, taking count of my condition, and ever present to notice my first sign of distress or need. He assigned Himself to me and to each of us personally, to see to it that we all make it through this world and it's throes victoriously. And He is faithfully staying with each of us to the very end of the mission, no matter what lies ahead.

David had it right when he wrote "The Lord is MY shepherd."

He understood it was personal and possessive....not distant or formal.

Today I can gladly say that same line with the same confidence David had. "The Lord is MY shepherd!!!"

The Lord is my shepherd; I shall not want.

Psalm 23:1

"It is finished!"

...those three words were the beginning of a new era.

"It is finished" sealed the fate of sin as a forever conquered foe and submerged death in an unrecoverable pit of defeat.

It banished the unbearable burden of performance and shattered the illusion of an unapproachable and unrelationable God.

Unleashing a tidal wave of forgiveness, it drenched the entire world in a fervent, never before felt, loving wave of grace.

Propelled by mercy's plea, it crushed the thorny curse of eternal separation, and birthed a new promise--bridled in the unbreakable vow of kinsmanship--of a royal heritage through adoption by blood.

And last it started the beginning of the end of that deceptive serpent's tyrannical reign of darkness and terror--his days became numbered.

Those three words ignited a chain reaction of change that can never be undone.

It's pulsating force is still being felt around the world and in the hearts of those around today.

The moment those three words were uttered, everything shifted.

Jesus saith unto him, I am the way, the truth, and the life: no man cometh unto the Father, but by me.

John 14:6

Jesus' grace isn't limited by the shallow depth of my cup.

His grace is limitless, overflowing, boundless, and ever abundant.
The cracks in my cup do not hinder His grace either.
For the cracks, to Him, mean that His grace can trickle down through my brokenness onto those around me.....touching their hearts in a way He alone can. And finally, the grace that leaves my cup through the broken places does not mean I'll be left dry and empty.....but rather, because of it He is ever faithful to see to it that I'm filled a new, topped off, and overflowing again. Not just so I can have a full cup all to myself, but so that I may continue to let His grace fall out of my cup onto those around me who are thirsty and in need of Him.

But in a great house there are not only vessels of gold and of silver, but also of wood and of earth; and some to honour, and some to dishonour. If a man therefore purge himself from these, he shall be a vessel unto honour, sanctified, and meet for the master's use, and prepared unto every good work.

2 Timothy 2:21

Growth.

Oftentimes it's measured by what we can see or understand.

Spring's first day was last month and all around me were vibrant colors and beautiful greens.

However, there was one tree that remained bare on that first day of spring.

In fact, it kept it's dead appearance way beyond the "hey winter is passed, didn't you get the memo?" announcement.

It actually threw off the spring vibe in the yard. It looked dead.....like no change was happening at all.

Then four weeks after the first day of spring, I saw this bud of hope burst forth. Growth had occurred and had been occurring all along, albeit I couldn't see it the weeks before.

My timing for this tree's growth was not fulfilled.

God knew that the first day of spring, however glamorous as it may have seemed, was not the best time for this tree to come to life again.

It needed to sit a little longer in a dormant state, going against all reason, in order to ensure a successful bloom. Any earlier and it would've failed.

Maybe you're there right now....seeing everyone else bloom around you but you're still stuck in winter. Let me encourage you, be patient in this dormant state.

He's working in you something that others may not be able to see right off. Oftentimes growth occurs beneath where others eyes can't reach.

In this quiet, barren state He's busy putting together all the necessary components needed to burst you through into the next stage.

It won't last forever, although it may feel like forever. It may feel lonely, uncertain, a little weird, and a bit out of place. However God knows exactly how long the process must be to produce in you the perfect bloom.

It may not be according to your family, friend's, or church's timing--or even your timing, but I assure you it will be in His perfect timing. So rest, be still, and let this state take it's full effect in you through His hands.

For my thoughts are not your thoughts, neither are your ways my ways, saith the Lord.

Isaiah 55:8

The world is constantly at work trying to tear down the truth "beautifully and wonderfully made". It has erected lies campaigning the themes "flawed in design", "a mistake", "needs to change", and "isn't worth more".
It has built an ever shifting standard, burdening the strong and weak alike. But a lie will eventually crumble and fall. That's why there is never any lasting self fulfillment in chasing this lie.
However, God's immovable truth of "beautifully and wonderfully made" is a bright beacon pointing directly to His heart.
That He lovingly and passionately fashioned every limb, aspect, gene, and quirk that makes us who we are. We weren't half baked, thrown together with leftovers, or outsourced to a lower paying company to do the job cheaper.
We were designed, not discounted....but that's what the world wants us to believe---that somehow we're flawed, secondhand store worthy at best.
Let's not believe a twisted lie from a world who will never love us unconditionally.
Instead, let's cling to the immovable truth spoken by a loving, ever head over heels for us, God.

Behold, I have graven thee upon the palms of
my hands

Isaiah 49:16

A little nugget of wisdom:

Temptation goes after the voids you have in your life.
It preys on them and formulates a delicious looking piece of fruit that promises to eliminate the void, or emptiness you feel inside.
Temptation uses the fruit to tantalize the person into believing that they have the power to make themselves whole again.
That they can fill any holes or pockets of emptiness themselves. That they are in control and know exactly what they need, how much, and when to stop.
For Eve, the fruit made her believe she would become wise because perhaps she felt inadequate with herself and less than....a void she believed she had.
For others, the fruit looks like the answer to finally finding intimacy and love, or maybe an answer to financial problems, or perhaps the feeling of fullness and self worth.
These tantalizing fruits lead people into adultery, financial schemes, impulse buying, and even substance abuse....just to name a few. And when the person declares they've had enough and want to change, the temptation leaves them but for a moment, knowing soon the void will beckon that piece of fruit to come back. And thus the cycle starts itself all over again.
The only One Who has ever defeated temptation is Jesus.
The only One Who can permanently fill every empty place in our heart is Jesus.
We were not created to fill our own holes.
We are not capable of filling our own voids.
We do not have what it takes to completely eliminate our emptiness or feelings of lack on our own.
Victorious living, free of constantly falling into the temptation cycle is only possible when we turn to Him and allow Him to completely fill our emptiness.
Once Jesus fills our emptiness, the tantalizing fruit will no longer appear delicious...for we will see it as it truly is, a disgusting rotting lie hanging on a dead and defeated tree.
So the next time that fruit looks so good, run fast to Jesus and away from the temptation.
Your life and the purpose you were created for depends on it.

There hath no temptation taken you but such as is common to man: but God is faithful, who will not suffer you to be tempted above that ye are able; but will with the temptation also make a way to escape, that ye may be able to bear it.

1 Corinthians 10:13

Spring reminds me of God's faithfulness.

Having gone through long, dark, cold winter nights, and days filled with barren trees and gray skies....my heart can finally breathe in the fresh crisp color of green leaves and my eyes can finally behold beautiful colors blooming all around...the joyous signs of new life are everywhere.

And with this new fragrant season upon us, I'm reminded of His faithful promise--to one day make all things new.

That promise blossomed on the thorns of a misshapen crown--worn by an absolute perfect Rose, who's crushed petals satisfied a debt owed by all.

So that one day we all could inherit the promise of a new life, a new heart, a new name, and a new home. No more thorns, no more tears, no more grey skies, and no more long dark, cold nights for the soul.

To me spring is a keyhole glimpse into God's faithful promise.

Behold, I will do a new thing; now it
shall spring forth; shall ye not know it? I
will even make a way in the wilderness,
and rivers in the desert.

Isaiah 43:19

I have heard it said that it's better to "eat to live" and not "live to eat".

That got me thinking.....

Although that approach is valid when speaking of our physical bodies, I don't believe that quote carries weight for our spiritual bodies.

For us to only eat or partake of God's Word, or nourishment, just so we can function well as a good Christian, loses the intimate act of savoring His Word through the worship of enjoyment.

You see, God wants us to not just consume His Word because we have to or are suppose to.

But rather to come to His Word to find enjoyment.

To savor the delicious and delicate notes of His essence throughout every page.

To stop, sit, and truly taste the sweet flavor of His masterpiece.

Slowly taking in the meaning of every ingredient, every word, and every passage....not just scarfing it down like a bowl of bran cereal before you dash out the door.

But rather like a huge slice of the best, creamiest cheesecake in which you seclude yourself in joyous desire--filled with unbearable anticipation of savoring every single morsel.

Savoring His Word brings enjoyment, which is a form of worship.

Let's strive to not only be consumers of His Word but savorers as well.

Thy word is a lamp unto my feet, and a light unto my path.

Psalm 119:105

A Word from the Author

"Finding delight in God's word is so vital to my walk. Savoring my time with Him, in the Word, sustains me through the day. Quieting myself and focusing my mind on the words before me can sometimes prove challenging. But like the blue birds in the morning, who wait patiently in expectation of sustenance, I too will continue to wait patiently for my spirit to be filled...to out wait my mind's desire to wonder-- that I may receive the fullness of His message without hindrance.

My hope for the reader is they will allow themselves to grow and blossom throughout every season of life. Fully yielding themselves to the Lord's pruning as they learn to abide in the Vine daily. Seizing the opportunity for the Lord to reveal Himself in every circumstance, whether good or bad.
And lastly, to receive Him into every part of our hearts and lives entirely."

---Hanna Lorraine

CPSIA information can be obtained
at www.ICGtesting.com
Printed in the USA
LVHW071143141019
634130LV00032B/8325/P